T0193833

Gentle
Whispers

B . Z . WINTERS

WESTBOW
PRESS®
A DIVISION OF THOMAS NELSON
& ZONDERVAN

WestBow Press books may be ordered through booksellers or by contacting:

WestBow Press
A Division of Thomas Nelson & Zondervan
1663 Liberty Drive
Bloomington, IN 47403
www.westbowpress.com
1 (866) 928-1240

Because of the dynamic nature of the Internet, any web addresses or
links contained in this book may have changed since publication and
may no longer be valid. The views expressed in this work are solely those
of the author and do not necessarily reflect the views of the publisher,
and the publisher hereby disclaims any responsibility for them.

Any people depicted in stock imagery provided by Getty Images are models,
and such images are being used for illustrative purposes only.
Certain stock imagery © Getty Images.

ISBN: 978-1-9736-5813-9 (sc)
ISBN: 978-1-9736-5812-2 (e)

Print information available on the last page.

WestBow Press rev. date: 04/01/2019

EDITOR

Editing by Reverend Michael Grant, B.A (Theology); M.A. (Bible and Family Life Education).

INTRODUCTION

Have you ever felt like a "nobody" in the eyes of society? Have you ever considered suicide, been a victim of different types of abuse, suffered through rejection, been treated unjustly, been betrayed by people close to you? You have been overwhelmed by pain if you have experienced any such adversity.

Well, well, you have chosen the right book. I know that the Master has led you here. In this book, I am going to show you how you can overcome all that injustice done to you, and enjoy peace that surpasses understanding. The "icing on the cake" is that it would cost you nothing financially to take this path.

I ask you to trust me on this because I have lived through all those negative experiences and more. Today, I live a transformed life and I know you can do it too.

Do you want to enjoy a better life? This

book, with many helpful hints, can greatly assist you.

I am living proof that what you read in this book is invaluable advice. I was inspired to write this book to help others, so that my living will not be in vain.

I can promise you that heeding my advice about complete surrender to God will bring eye-opening transformation in your life.

Do not wait a minute longer to learn how you can overcome the obstacles in your life and how God can use you to inspire others. He is awaiting you with open arms because He loves you.

Like me, you are a "whosoever" as described in the words of Jesus, the Christ (John3:16 – King James Version) – For God so loved the world, that He gave His only begotten Son, that whosoever believeth in Him should not perish, but have everlasting life.

EPIGRAPH

"The world is like a mountain.
Your echo depends on you.
If you scream good things,
the world will give it back.
If you scream bad things,
the world will give it back.
Even if someone says badly about you,
speak well about him.
Change your heart to change the world.

(Shams Tabrizi – Persian Instructor)

DEDICATION

This book is dedicated to all those who aspire for greater peace in their lives, to give hope to the hopeless, and courage to the discouraged.

ACKNOWLEDGEMENT

I am grateful to my daughter, Camille, who assisted me with preparation of my manuscript on the computer, and my son, Garrick, for his support. He has suggested to me that I should record all my testimonies of God's grace and favor in my life. That would be another book.

I am grateful also to Reverend Michael Grant and his wife, Annel, for their invaluable support and encouragement with this project.

I am thankful to my dear friend, Nadira, who was instrumental in my journey to become a follower of Jesus, the Christ.

CONTENTS

(I am a) Whosoever 1

Washed But Not "Washed Up" 6

Feel Good or Do Good 9

Love Letters 13

From Rejection to Celebration 17

The Valley of Growth and Education 20

God is the Best Business Partner 23

No More a Slave 27

It's Not All About Me (Or You) 31

Worship, Worship, Worship 36

Sharing His Blessings with Others 41

All In 44

You Are One of a Kind 48

Lemonade Anyone? 52

A Different View of Judas 54

Open 24/7 57

PREFACE

This book was inspired by God, through a Nigerian Pastor Sam Adeyemi who, in my opinion, is a masterful communicator. I know he spoke to me as a messenger of our Lord, through one of his sermons on television, while I pondered my next step in life.

Pastor Adeyemi spoke of the blessings God has bestowed on us through gifts and talents. We are expected to utilize these gifts and talents in accordance with His will for the greater good of mankind.

We should therefore, in oneness with God, identify our gifts and passions and determine how we can be most effective in making a difference in the lives of others. Obviously, our gifts should be utilized appropriately to reflect God's glory.

This is my first book and my desire is that, with God's grace, many persons will be encouraged to seek a more intimate relationship with our Lord and God who is the Author and Finisher of our faith. No matter what type of beginnings we experienced, we can choose to have a great ending and to spend eternity with our Lord.

(I AM A) WHOSOEVER

M any of us have heard the old adage, "Experience is the best teacher." Sometimes I wonder if our Creator's plan is to have a person born into a certain family, in a particular environment, to live through experiences, which help us to have tremendous empathy and a willingness to assist others with similar negative occurrences.

In accordance with societal standards, it happens often that one born into impoverished circumstances, suffered through different types of abuse in a very dysfunctional family, will exhibit very low self-esteem and become an introvert. When such a person suffers rejection from non-family members, it is difficult to operate on an even playing field with peers. Typically, this person will feel like a "nobody" in the eyes of the society.

In addition to the above, imagine feeling so confused (and invisible) as to why my older relatives will visit my family home of thirteen children, and looking at me, just me, will question, "Who is this girl? I don't know her. I know the older ones and the younger ones, but I don't know her."

Talk about feeling like a "nobody?" For a great part of my life, this has been my experience.

I must state that for so many years, I did not believe that God really existed. I could not understand why innocent children born into this world would be subjected to different types of abuse, and if God exists, He does not intervene.

I was so sick of being sick with the abuses in my life but did not know what to do. As I look at my situation in retrospect, I realize that God sent a dog into my life then, to begin His transforming work in my life. This event caused me to start a conversation with my hairdresser. My delight in informing her about the aforementioned dog was the first lengthy communication I had with her after being her client for eight years. That is an indication of how sick I was of the mess my life had been. I had no interest in conversing with anyone beyond what was necessary to be said. God used my passion for animals to get me on the road to healing. She invited me to attend her church and when I eventually did so, it was the beginning of a new journey.

It was then that I was first exposed to teachings about the Holy Spirit. Prior to that time, whenever I attended a church service, I got the impression that only the church Ministers were able to have a personal relationship with our God. I accepted Jesus, the Christ, as my Lord and Savior. I was baptized as is the custom, and invited the presence of the Holy Spirit in my life.

Sometime after that event, I recall a pastor asking the congregation about the difference in our lives, prior to, and after the experience of baptism in the Spirit. I did not even need to think about that. It was uppermost in my mind. Prior to that experience, I always felt so alone, a "nobody," with all these dreadful secrets of abuse and rejections that I could not tell to anyone. After that experience, I have never felt alone. I know that the Holy Spirit lives in me and is my constant companion. He is my protector, my guide, my counselor, among many other things. I am confident that I belong in God's family.

Possibly the most popular verse in the Bible is quoted from the gospel of John 3:16 (King James Version) - "For God so loved the world that he gave his only begotten Son, that WHOSOEVER believeth in him shall not perish but have everlasting life."

Sometime ago, I began to sense what I perceive to be "Gentle Whispers" or "Spiritual Promptings" from the Holy Spirit, pertaining to enlightenment about certain topics. The first, I recall, is the importance of the word "WHOSOEVER" in the above quoted scripture that gives great validity to people with my experiences. The Lord's grace has put us all on a level playing field and we need not satisfy any societal requirements or qualifications to receive His grace, if we so desire.

God created us all and He does not discriminate like some people do. So whether we are rich or poor, privileged or underprivileged, educated or uneducated, whatever our ethnic origin, a "somebody" or a "nobody" in the eyes of the world, we are all equal in His eyes. We all qualify for the gift of salvation and eternal life if we so choose. It is now up to us, to believe in the Christ, to publicly declare His Lordship over our lives by being baptized in the Holy Spirit, and to seek His assistance in transforming our lives.

The best part of all is that this gift of salvation is exactly what it is, a gift, meaning no monetary costs are necessary, so all "nobodies" have the opportunity to become joint heirs with Jesus to the royal throne of God.

One thing we are certain of, is that our Lord will never reject us as some in the society do. Is that not wonderful to know? No matter how we are treated by the society, our Lord validates and accepts us. What better gift can we ask for?

I can certainly declare that this "nobody" in the society's view, has definitely realized that I am a "WHOSOEVER," and I now feel like a princess, a daughter of the most high King. Jesus, the Christ, gives hope to the hopeless, and love to the unloved. Accept JESUS as Savior and friend.

WASHED BUT NOT
"WASHED UP"

I faintly remember an ageless hymn, "Come as you are," which indicates that Jesus has invited us all to come to Him as we are, no matter what our circumstances may be. This invitation goes out to all and sundry, including the broken spirited, the hopeless, the despaired, the criminals, prisoners, etc. No matter what sins we have committed, our Lord waits for us with open arms.

Jesus has promised that if we believe that He is the Christ and we accept His invitation to receive salvation through faith, we can seek repentance for all our sins from God, the Father. The grace and mercy of God will wash away our sins when we make our request in the name of His Son, Jesus.

In the secular world, many believe that if you have messed up in life, e.g. if you have committed crimes and even ended up in prison; if you are an addict of sorts and brought destruction to your families and relationships; if you have been promiscuous; if you have a terrible attitude and have mistreated people all your life; if you conduct your life without a moral compass, that the only way forward is lower and lower into a pit. Such a person is sometimes described as "washed up," meaning that you are condemned by the society.

To the contrary, our merciful and loving God desires to have an intimate relationship with all of mankind. He is our creator and He knows all our weaknesses, the wrong choices we have made and will make, the temptations that challenge us daily, and all sins that we have committed. God's love is unconditional and through His Son, Jesus, the Christ, He made provision for our redemption and to restore relationship with us.

God could have given us no greater gift than that of His Son, the Christ, who, when He was crucified, took upon Himself all our sins. His blood that was shed is the cleansing agent that washes away our sins if we accept Him as our Savior. Jesus tells us that He is the way, the truth, and the life. No one comes to the Father except through Him. (John 14:6 – New Living Translation). Hence the reason we sing of "The Cleansing Blood," and "We Are Washed In The Blood."

Ultimately, each person can choose to either be "Washed In The Blood" or be "Washed Up."

FEEL GOOD OR DO GOOD

Most of us know that not every action that we indulge in that feels good to us may necessarily be good for us. This does not only relate to "religious" people but also the secular world.

For example, if a person likes the taste of ice-cream very much, and chooses to consume just ice-cream to quell hunger three times a day, instead of nutritious meals, over a period of time, naturally his body would suffer the consequences of a lack of a balanced diet. Although the ice-cream would have satisfied his palate at the time of consumption, the after effects are what would then pose great challenges to his health.

Similarly, our spiritual lives require constant checks and balances to ensure that we are living our lives in accordance with the teachings of our Lord and Savior, Jesus Christ.

As we've heard it said countless times, "Life

is no bed of roses." There is no guarantee that a person who has consecrated his life to God, endeavoring to conform to the likeness of His Son, Jesus, will not be challenged by emotions of the flesh.

We are only in control of our own words and actions and not the actions of others. What is important is how we choose to respond to the words and actions of others that affect us. Jesus has taught us that many persecutions:-betrayals, discriminatory practices, bullying, natural disasters, assaults, theft of earthly possessions, acts of hate as a result of envy, etc. will come our way.

Our Lord has also advised us on how we should respond to all the negativity perpetrated against us. He has clearly said that He is our vindicator and we should totally leave those issues up to Him. Isn't it comforting to know that our Savior, our big brother, our loyal friend, would fight for us?

Our greatest challenge therefore, is not letting our fleshly emotions to get the better of us.

We are human beings and it is only natural that we experience great hurt and judgment when we are persecuted for no reason. This is especially so when the persons who betray our trust are those who are close to us.

Our natural reactions are to confront the perpetrator of the injustice and let him know he has hurt our feelings. We also want the world to know how this person has hurt us.

God's grace can substantially assist us in extending forgiveness to the perpetrator, however, this does not instantly eradicate our feelings of hurt. In instances where criminal acts are committed, forgiving the perpetrator is really beneficial for us, the victims, as then we are no longer burdened with unforgiveness.

Forgiveness does not necessarily transform the life of the perpetrator, so the matter of trust is another issue, and therefore we cannot assume that the person will not hurt us in the future.

My personal experience with this "Feel Good Or Do Good" theme occurred when a close relative betrayed my trust and continued to persecute me by making false allegations against me. This was very hurtful to me, however, after some time, I was able to forgive that person and pray for her salvation and transformation of her life. We must always remember to leave vindication to God.

I was preparing to attend a family gathering where I knew that I would see my persecutor. A thought entered my mind that if she attempted to converse with me, I should respond with a sarcastic remark. Immediately I sensed a gentle whisper from the Holy Spirit saying to me, "That would feel good to you, wouldn't it? Think about it, do you want to feel good or do good?" I must say that I chose to DO GOOD and no sarcasm was involved.

LOVE LETTERS

Isn't it just so awesome that our Master Creator loves us all so much that He has made available to us a compilation of Love Letters known as "The Bible?" He has inspired these Love Letters for all of His children, no matter who you are or where you are.

Once we are exposed to God's Love Letters, and we elect to read and pore over same, it is observed that He addresses every issue in this world. He tells us about His creation of the universe for us because He loves us so much. He emphasizes the fact that He loves us all, whether or not we return His love, and of course, we know this love as unconditional love.

Our Master Creator gives us guidance as to how we should live our lives so that we will not be self-destructive. He also advises us how we should treat the environment we live in, so that we will not destroy same. Our loving

God instructs us how we should interact with mankind so that an atmosphere of peace and calm is maintained.

We can read of a very detailed history in The Old Testament and as a result, we can avoid making similar mistakes that others did in the past. We can observe His "hands on" relationship with several persons in The Old Testament whom He inspired to tell their fellowman of His great love for all. In spite of this, much sin still did abound.

In The New Testament, our Master Creator spares no effort to exhibit His love for us all. There is no greater sacrifice He could have made than to send His Son, Jesus, the Christ, to die, to shed His blood, to be an innocent sinless lamb who was crucified, so that His blood can wash away the stains of our sins. Followers of Jesus can be redeemed and restore an intimate relationship with Our Father, our dear loving God, if we so choose.

Our Master Creator goes to great lengths to motivate us with a history of the miracles He can perform to better our lives. We are flooded with numerous parables and testimonies of those who existed in Biblical times of God's supernatural grace and favor, and His mercies which endure forever. His inspired letters tell us of His infinite patience while He waits for us to come to Him by choice, to be fully enveloped in His Lordship over our lives.

We are made aware that the Holy Spirit, if we accept His invitation, lives in us, and is our constant companion, guide, comforter, and counselor. We can experience a sense of Peace which surpasses understanding. We can seek the assistance of the Holy Spirit to transform our lives and to aspire to be clothed with the beauty of the Christ so that others can see Him when they see us. We can become lamps in the paths of others.

God's inspired letters also give us a glimpse of the end times, the battle between good and evil. Regardless of what a person thinks of God and His unparalleled love for us, we can be sure of at least one thing, that our Creator keeps His promises to us. He has gracefully and lovingly extended His invitation to us all to join Him in Eternity.

Our Creator has also given us a commission, asking us to partner with Him to convey the Good News of the Gospel to the ends of the earth. We are well aware that the Gospel has not yet reached some of God's children. Our love for our Lord can be manifested in several ways, one of which can be to carry out this Great Commission.

Our loving Father wishes that all would return His love and live in His presence, however, He has advised us that we are free to choose our path. He waits with open arms to embrace us if we opt for his supernatural love and goodness, grace and favor.

FROM REJECTION
TO CELEBRATION

It is a fact that when we come into this world, we do so without having a choice in our beginnings. We could not choose the family we are born into, the circumstances surrounding that family, the advantages or disadvantages we are faced with, while we struggle to acquire some perspective on Life itself. There is so much that we are unable to understand or explain.

Our Creator selects the circumstances of our beginnings. He alone knows why some are born into privileged circumstances with abundant resources and facilities afforded them throughout their lives. Others are born into less fortunate economic circumstances and life is a continuous struggle to survive. Some are born into extreme adversity like famine, raging war, a total lack of the basic necessities to even survive. Others are born to rejection from parents and are either abandoned or given up for adoption. Some are born into families with such severe dysfunction and abuse taking place, that the challenges to be confronted are enormous. A person from such a background is vulnerable to persons outside of the home and may experience even more abuse and rejection.

In addition to being born into underprivileged circumstances, many people are subjected to rejection in the social sphere. Certain standards are established by the society, and if one does not meet those standards, he can be rejected and considered inferior.

Oh, but for the supernatural saving grace and favor of our God. As He tells us in His word, He blessed us when we were yet sinners, and waits for us to come to Him, believing in Him, having faith in Him, being obedient to His Word, and trusting Him. God has promised us that He will never leave us nor forsake us, and that we are joint heirs with Jesus, the Christ, in His kingdom.

God has assured us that we will receive beauty for ashes, that He will restore what was stolen from us, several times over. We must remember, however, that we should have the capability to receive the beauty by first releasing all the ashes.

THE VALLEY OF GROWTH AND EDUCATION

It is natural to feel overwhelmed and depressed when we are challenged with adversities, which can be described as being "in the valley." We should not, however, beat ourselves over the head for feeling that way. We are likely to start thinking that life is not fair as we ponder the fact that we have endeavored to be obedient and faithful to our God.

It would be beneficial to us when we start viewing these experiences in a different light. Think of the analogy of when you were being educated in the academics, or even in other areas. Occasionally you would be tested or examined to determine your eligibility to move to a higher level.

Similarly, our Lord God needs to test us from time to time to assess the level of our commitment to Him and our spirituality.

Having faith in Jesus avails us of an advantage when we are faced with adversities. We are blessed with His grace to endure the experience. Whether we realize it or not, He is there in the valley with us, overseeing our testing process and witnessing the development of our spiritual muscles. He tends not to interrupt the process except if we are really drowning in the sea of adversity. Think of a parent teaching a child to ride a tricycle.

When the valley experience then transitions to a more favorable period of life, we can then totally appreciate the spiritual muscles we have developed while we endured the challenges.

Psalm 34:19-20 (New Living Translation) states that:

> "The righteous face many troubles,
> but the Lord rescues them from
> each and every one, for the Lord
> protects them from harm, not one
> of their bones will be broken."

While we are in the valley, another comforting scripture we can meditate on is

Romans 8:28 (New Living Translation) "And we know that God causes everything to work together for the good of those who love God and are called according to his purpose for them."

Our Lord knows that a person's character can only be developed in the tough times (in the valley) when we struggle with mountainous challenges. This is when our level of faith in our God can be increased. When our situations in the valley appear to be extremely bleak (in the natural) and we are unable to see any solutions on the horizon, we have no choice but to rely on the mercy, the supernatural grace and supernatural favor of our God. Many a time He will bless us with His miraculous solutions at the eleventh hour, having stretched us to the limit, and oh how His glory shines through. The Lord likes to toughen us up in preparation for what lies ahead of us.

While we are in the valley, God is honored when we embrace where we are, continue to do what is right, while maintaining a good attitude. This is conducive to our achieving our divine purpose.

GOD IS THE BEST BUSINESS PARTNER

In the natural, a partnership is an association between individuals or companies entered into, for commercial purposes. Each partner would normally bring some form of capital to the table e.g. financial resources, time, knowledge, and skills, in pursuit of a shared vision.

Partners would mutually own, manage, and create a company. In such a setting, no one person will need to make major decisions alone.

For Christians who choose to have God as a business partner, the structure of this association is a different one from that of the natural.

Our wonderful God has great riches, wisdom, and knowledge. He brings all the resources to the table. A God partner has the role of a steward, which means that you have a say, but only in light of God's purposes and goals. You do your part, but God is really in control. You play a role, but it is a supporting one. One advantage of having God as your partner, is avoiding problems inherent in a natural business partnership.

Partnering with God encompasses so much more than managing material resources. You have heard it said that we are God's hands, feet, and mouth on the earth.

When God wants to accomplish a job on earth, He speaks to His partners' hearts and minds and by "Gentle Whispers." He would be so delighted if one hundred per cent of the time, His requests are obeyed and carried out without any questioning and deliberations from us, His partners. Sometimes it is difficult and may even seem impossible for us to understand His decisions and His methods to be used to carry out a task.

"Oh my people, trust in him at all times. Pour out your heart to him, for God is our refuge," (Psalm 62:8 - New Living Translation) advised King David, whom God described as a man after His own heart.

Many people have either read or heard of the prophet, Jonah, in the Old Testament, and what is most remembered is that Jonah was swallowed by a great fish. After three days in the belly of the fish, God ordered the fish to spit out Jonah where he would be safe.

This unusual experience came about when Jonah disobeyed God's instructions and was running from His presence. God had asked His earthly partner, Jonah, to go to the city of Nineveh and preach repentance to the people as they led wicked and sinful lives. Jonah was not in favor of God relenting and being merciful to the Ninevites. Jonah got on a ship travelling in the opposite direction, to Tarshish.

During a violent storm on that journey, Jonah confessed to the crew that he was running from God. They hesitantly threw him into the sea and he ended up in the fish's belly. After being spit out on land, God again directed Jonah to Nineveh to accomplish His goal. Jonah obeyed and the Ninevites repented and escaped God's judgment.

The emphasis here is that when we partner with God, we should trust Him totally. He is prepared to go to great lengths to achieve His purposes. We should not be judgmental about

God's mercy and grace to anyone, no matter how we feel about the situation.

We should also be mindful of the fact that when we partner with God, we may suffer rejection, especially from those who are close to us. We may be the victims of mockery and insults. We may experience persecution when lies are fabricated about us.

We should find comfort in the gospel of Matthew 5: 11-12 (New Living Translation), "God blesses you when you are mocked and persecuted and lied about, because you are my followers. Be happy about it! Be very glad! For a great reward awaits you in heaven. And remember the ancient prophets were persecuted, too."

Should we not feel honored and humbled when the Lord chooses us as earthly partners to get His work done?

NO MORE A SLAVE

We have heard it said that where and how you started in life is not nearly as important as how you finish or reaching your destiny. After all, Jesus, the son of God, was born in a manger, wrapped in swaddling clothes, experienced severe persecution for doing good and eventually crucified. He now sits on the right hand of God, the Father Almighty.

Although we cannot choose our beginnings, and maybe our "middle," we do enjoy a privilege, to a certain extent, to opt for our destiny.

We can choose to believe God when He says that what others meant for harm when they perpetrated certain actions against us, He will turn it around for our good.

A prominent example of God's power in such matters is manifested in the story of Joseph, in the Old Testament (Genesis). Joseph was envied by his brothers when he told them of his dreams where they were bowing down to him.

The brothers threw him into a pit, hoping to be rid of him. At that time some Ishmaelite traders came along and the brothers opted to make some money by selling Joseph as a slave, and he was taken to Egypt. He was then sold to a senior Egyptian official, whose wife wrongfully accused Joseph of raping and assaulting her, and he was sent to prison.

While in prison, the chief jailer put Joseph in charge of the other prisoners, and all operations where he learned management skills. Some time later, Joseph was summoned by Pharoah to interpret his dreams and then he was appointed Prime Minister of Egypt. What Joseph's brothers meant for harm, God turned his situation around for good.

We can choose to believe that God's supernatural grace can transform our lives and empower us to get rid of thoughts of mental slavery.

We can ignore the voices from the past (and possibly present), which tell us that we are: useless; we have no ability to realize our dreams; we will never amount to anything significant; we belong on "the wrong side of the tracks"; we were not born to influential families so we cannot achieve anything in life; we are not educated enough.

We should be mindful of the fact that there are some people around us who would be only too happy to keep us oppressed and suppressed all our lives. They would do anything in their power to deter us from flourishing.

We can drown out the naysayers by frequently articulating God's promises to all mankind in His inspired Word, the Bible. We can exercise our faith in God by pursuing our dreams without bowing to distractions. Once we have established an intimate relationship with our Lord, and we endeavor to live our lives to reflect His glory, we cannot be separated from Him.

When we make decisions to follow Jesus, we need to stand strong, regardless of the challenges that confront us. We may lose the support of most or all our friends and relatives, face mockery and sarcasm etc. We need to remember that those persons were happier while we exhibited a mentality of slavery. They may be envious of the fact that we have mustered the strength by working in tandem with the Holy Spirit to transform our lives from victims to victors.

IT'S NOT ALL ABOUT
ME (OR YOU)

Normally, when we are faced with challenges in life, we can come up with a long list of questions for God. We may ask:-

Why me, God?

What did I do to deserve this?

When will this situation be resolved?

What do you want me to learn from this experience?

Why am I going through this 'valley' when I have endeavored to be obedient to you, trying to walk in the footsteps of Jesus, and attempting to lead a blameless life like Noah?

We may actually view the situation, when it is ended, as so unnecessary, so far-fetched from what we think our spiritual journey should be, such a waste of time. Little do we realize that God is working with us to accomplish his purpose here on earth.

It is possible that God is preparing us in a certain situation for events that may occur in the future, and then we will better be able to handle a similar future challenge. In "2 Corinthians, Chap. 1, Verses 3-4" (New Living Translation), the apostle, Paul states: "All praise to the God and Father of our Lord Jesus Christ. He is the source of every mercy and the God who comforts us. He comforts us in all our troubles so that we can comfort others. When others are troubled, we will be able to give them the same comfort God has given us."

We may also feel spiritually led in a certain direction, and we go willingly and obediently. Shortly after we are in the position we felt led to, we feel disappointed, uncomfortable, inconvenienced, and that this is not our 'cup of tea'.

In the natural, we may even entertain

thoughts of removing ourselves from that position, however, we may feel confused as to why we were led there in the first place. We then experience a sense of being 'boxed in'.

When we are confused, the best choice we can make is to seek the counseling of the Holy Spirit on the matter. It might be surprising to us to learn that we were led to where we are, not for our benefit, but to assist or to impact others in that environment.

When we become enlightened in this manner, we then experience a greater sense of peace as we have a true perspective of the matter at hand.

Sometimes, God will put on our hearts to comply with His request to perform a task that may seem quite ridiculous to onlookers. For example, when God asked Noah (Genesis) to build an ark, the people mocked and jeered at him as it had not rained for such a long time and there was no indication that they will see rain in the near future. They could not imagine an ark being necessary at that time. As biblical history tells us, the ark served God's purpose to save Noah and his family when He sent rain and floods to destroy the earth.

It is important for us to obey God's directives, no matter how ridiculous it appears to the natural world.

Occasionally, we may sense a prompting from the Holy Spirit to bless someone, or a family by paying for their groceries; paying the bill for someone's lunch or dinner; purchasing an item that someone needs urgently but cannot afford it. We may feel a bit awkward when those persons are strangers and we are not sure what the response will be. We may experience doubts that God is speaking to us and not heed His call.

God seeks willing hearts to carry out His purposes on this earth, no matter how "strange" or "odd" we appear to others.

Some time ago, I was at a grocery checkout counter when I heard one of the packers at another counter telling his colleagues that he was celebrating his birthday on that day. I sensed in my spirit that I should give him some cash to purchase a nice birthday lunch. I did not do so because I did not want the birthday guy and his colleagues to think that

I was "crazy" or "weird" or something of that nature.

At that time I forgot to collect my driver's permit identification, which I had used with my credit card, from the cashier. Two days later, I discovered the driver's permit was missing and I checked with the grocery where I last used it. The permit was in their possession and I had to return to the grocery to collect same. The uppermost issue in my mind was that I should have given the financial gift to the young man, and here was another chance to do so, because the directive came from the Holy Spirit.

Although the young man was not on duty when I went to collect my document, I left the gift with his supervisor to pass on to him.

I am convinced that I forgot my document on that day so that I needed to return to do what I should have done on the young man's birthday.

WORSHIP, WORSHIP, WORSHIP

M any of us think of singing slow songs in church when we speak of worship. It is, of course, just one aspect of the full meaning of worship.

The Webster Dictionary defines worship as follows:-

Worship is to honor with extravagant love and extreme submission.

We sing several songs about the worthiness of God and if we truly believe in our hearts that He is worthy of our total submission to Him, then the practice of worship should be easier.

As Christians, worship of our God should be our way of life, our everyday life, not only in the church building, but even more importantly, our every action outside of the church building. What we should aim at, is to live a lifestyle of holiness.

We should worship God with such a lifestyle because of our love and adoration of Him and not that we feel mandated to do so. When we accept the Lord Jesus Christ as our Savior, we ought to grow into the fullness of our salvation, since we have tasted of the Lord's goodness and kindness.

Once we are "born again," The Holy Spirit empowers us to transform our lifestyles, if we so desire. When we experience this alteration in our lives, that is, having no further interest in doing some things we did in the past, but only wanting to worship God with our new lifestyle, we know that we have taken "the narrow road".

When we think of two persons who love and adore each other very much, they are inclined to want to do things that are pleasing to each other. They do so out of great love for each other and not because they feel mandated to do so.

So too, the conduct of our lives should honor and worship God, because of our love and total submission to Him.

The Bible gives us tremendous guidance as

to how we can live a lifestyle of worship of our God. Here are some of my favorites:-

Keep your tongue from speaking evil.

Turn from evil and do good.

Work hard at living at peace with others.

The eyes of the Lord watch over those who do right, and His ears are open to their prayers.

The Lord turns His face against those who do evil.

Be gentle and respectful to others.

Humble yourself under the mighty power of God, and in His good time, He will honor you.

Manage the spiritual gifts God has blessed you with, so that His generosity can flow through you.

Give all your worries and cares to God, for He cares about what happens to you.

Be a light unto the world so you can assist in eliminating the darkness.

All of the aforementioned are conducive to honoring and worshipping God with our new lifestyles.

I have adopted a simple test that I apply if I am doubtful about a particular action, that has no definite biblical instruction about it.

I imagine myself sitting on a bench out in the garden, with Jesus sitting beside me. I relate my deliberation to Him and ask His advice on the matter. Should I or should I not do a particular action?

I sense that Jesus always reminds me that I know His teachings, and I know Him intimately. If I am at peace with a particular deed, I know it is the right thing to do. If I am not at peace with same, I should refrain from doing so.

We are aware therefore, that every thought

we have, every utterance we make, and every act we undertake, should be one of worship of our God. Would it not be awesome to walk in the footsteps of Jesus, the Christ? Oh how fascinating it can be when we imagine Him smiling down at us!

SHARING HIS BLESSINGS WITH OTHERS

We are all familiar with the saying, "God is good," and most of us will agree that this is true. God, however, does not bless us with abundance so that we can be rich fools.

Jesus gave an illustration on this topic in the form of a parable, Luke (Ch. 12 - New Living Translation). A rich man was blessed with an abundance of crops from his fertile farm, and his barns were overflowing with his harvest. This rich man did not entertain any thought of assisting the less fortunate with his excess. He made plans to tear down his barns to construct larger barns to accommodate all of his harvest.

This rich fool was then informed by God that he will die that very night. Then who will inherit his riches? This man obviously did not have an intimate relationship with our Lord, so he did not consider the fact that he should act responsibly and generously with his abundance, and not be greedy.

Should we though wait until we are blessed with abundance before we extend some assistance to our neighbors? Of course not! There are numerous ways in which we can make a positive difference in the lives of others, without having great abundance.

God's inspired word (the Bible) advises that we should care for widows and orphans in their troubles (James 1:27 – New Living Translation). You are probably in possession of a motor vehicle and you can offer to provide transport to a widow (who has no vehicle) to get her groceries or to run an errand.

You might know of a single mom who is needy, and surprise her and her kids with a pizza when you have been out treating your family to same.

You can cover the cost of grocery items for someone at the checkout counter if you see the person struggling to come up with the funds for his few items purchased.

You can offer to cook a meal for someone who lives alone and has a challenge with the use of their hands or feet.

The suggestions above do not require a lot from us, but would make such a difference in the lives of the persons on the receiving end. There is nothing to compare with the fulfillment you experience when you satisfy such a need.

There are many items we possess that we do not or will never utilize, and we know of someone who will love to have those items. Would it not be great to put a smile on someone's face by gifting the items to that person?

We will discover that life can be so simple when we adopt the motto:-

> 'Do unto others as you would
> have them do unto you'.

This will result in a very impactful lifestyle.

ALL IN

"I surrender all
I surrender all
All to thee my blessed savior
I surrender all,"
is the chorus of a song we often sing in Church with so much passion.

This begs the question, "Are we really sincere when we give voice to those words?" Even though at the time we sing that, we have not yet surrendered all to our Lord, are we endeavoring to do so by seeking the assistance of the Holy Spirit? It is definitely an ongoing challenge.

I have realized that life is a lot less complicated when we have firmly decided to make our Lord, Jesus, the focus of our lives.

This is not to say that we are exempt from having to confront challenges. Once we have an intimate relationship with our Lord, we can rely on the fact that His grace will empower us to go through the valleys of our challenges. We know that we are not alone on these journeys of testing.

Once we have made the decision to follow Jesus, and to surrender totally to Him, our interests and lifestyles will be altered. We need to be prepared for comments and criticism from some family members and friends. If they are not interested in pursuing a close relationship with Jesus, we may be described as extremists, odd, "a little too far out there," and similar statements.

Our faith in our Lord, however, keeps us grounded and on track. Is it not awesome to know that our Lord and Savior is on our side, encouraging us, consoling us, never leaving us?

Some people do not understand when you extend yourself to a great limit to lend a helping hand to others without any expectation of compensation. Some may refer to you as naïve, or may misinterpret your kindness for stupidity. We ought not be deterred by such thinking.

We know that Jesus went about doing good, and if we want to emulate Him, we should adopt this attitude as a lifestyle. After all, God has invited us to share eternal life with Him.

What good though, will it do to be a "lukewarm Christian?" This is when we are very good with the rituals of religion. We frequent the church services and impress our religious leaders, but how do we behave when we are not in church, and out of earshot of our "shepherds?"

Do we operate with integrity when no one else is around?

Are we respectful to all those with whom we interact?

Do we treat others as we would have them treat us?

Do we make Jesus the centre of our life, and consult Him first when we are faced with a challenge?

Do we do all in our power to pursue peace even when we are confronted by those persons who bring out the worst in us (sandpaper people)?

Do we do "tit for tat" when someone does something to hurt us? Do we attempt to get even or do we leave vindication up to the Lord?

All of the above relate to situations we encounter in our everyday life, and if we choose to respond as Jesus would in these matters, we will soon discover that life is a lot less complicated.

We know for a fact that there is a lot of darkness in this world. We also know that in His inspired word, God advises us to be lights in the world. Any person who has opted to follow Jesus, is a light unto the darkness. After all, we know that just one lit candle can provide so much light to an entirely dark room.

Imagine the impact we can have in this world if all Christians are "all in" for Jesus and we are the brightest shining lights God created us to be.

I consider it an unspeakable honor to be a child of God and a co-heir with Jesus Christ Should we not do our utmost to live our everyday lives in a manner that is worthy of this great honor?

YOU ARE ONE OF A KIND

It is so easy to be a people pleaser and follow the crowd. Some of us are so obsessed with "fitting in" with the crowd that we do not even think for ourselves anymore. We do not stop to think about whether we are happy or not, feeling fulfilled with our lifestyles or not.

For many years, I lived that lifestyle, not knowing any better, and was so very unhappy and confused as to why I am not happy and fulfilled.

What a revelation it was for me when I was fully enlightened about our gracious and merciful Lord with whom I can have an intimate relationship. When we believe in the Lord Jesus Christ, and we have faith and totally trust in Him, we are empowered by the Holy Spirit, who lives in us, to transform our lifestyles.

We can be transformed from people pleasers to God pleasers. We are then enabled to adopt lifestyles to follow in the footsteps of our Lord Jesus Christ. This transformation empowers us to be happy and comfortable "being ourselves" and living our lives with the leading of the Holy Spirit. We no longer are concerned with "fitting in" with the crowd.

This transition in our lives will gradually lead to revelations by the Holy Spirit of our various spiritual gifts and as to the roles designated for us as ambassadors of God on this earth. He is our Master and He is seeking willing hearts to carry out His purpose in this world. We must realize that our plans are subject to His plans and we are advised to "bloom where we are planted."

Our manner of dress would reflect what is pleasing to us and our Lord. The type of social entertainment we choose to engage in, may be different to what we did previously, however, we will experience a great sense of peace with our choices.

We experience a great sense of fulfillment when we indulge in elevating the lives of the less fortunate.

We feel free to first consult with our Lord

when we are faced with a challenge, which, if overwhelming, we can pray and leave it at the foot of the cross.

We develop a lifestyle of praise and thankfulness to God for all the miracles we experience every day, as a result of His supernatural grace and favor.

This new lifestyle is developed gradually and then we review our lives in its entirety, and wonder about how we got from where we were (following the crowd) to where we are presently (putting a large smile on the face of our Lord).

There are invaluable benefits made available to us when we consecrate our lives to the Lord Jesus and the Holy Spirit dwells within us. We are better managers of our everyday lives as we operate from a platform of peacefulness. We are empowered to respond to our challenges with wisdom meted out by the Holy Spirit. We conduct ourselves from a position of strength.

The more we educate ourselves with God's word, the more encouraged we are to do self introspection to discover the gifts with which we have been bestowed. Our gifts are to be shared with the world, and to impact and better the lives of others.

A true follower of Jesus will experience a sense of boldness in his approach to life. He is willing to explore his creativity that would enable him to be, and make positive changes in this world.

A strong and dedicated Christian should also expect criticism and snide remarks from some folks you would have socialized with previously. As sensitive human beings, a level of disappointment may set in when you realize that not all of your friends or family members are happy to see you progress in life. They will not admit that they are envious of your strength in taking such a stance, however, they find it easier to criticize your actions.

The most important thing to remember is that our Savior is in your corner, and you should not be bothered by negativity. Adherence to your decision becomes easier with time.

LEMONADE ANYONE?

We are quite familiar with the saying, "When life gives you lemons, make lemonade."

This quote is meant to inspire and motivate us when we are faced with mountainous challenges. These times may be described as the "dark periods" in our lives.

It is well known that lemons are generally sour tasting to the palate. When other ingredients are added to the juice of the lemons, it can be transformed into a sweetened beverage, a very refreshing drink, which quenches thirst.

So too, we can view the adversities in our lives with optimism. These are the times that really put us to the test. We use initiative and become quite creative. We may develop new skills and discover latent talents that we may possess.

The dark challenging times in our lives

can be seen as "spiritual set up" times. Our successful navigation of these "valleys" can be a springboard to a much more favorable future.

One of the happiest times of my life was several years ago when my job required my posting to a rural area for a period of two weeks. There was no television in the quarters where I stayed, at that time (lemons).

I have always been a voracious reader, and my work office was situated directly across the street from the village library. Needless to say, I made maximum use of that library during that time. Most of my non-working hours were spent reading (devouring) books.

I read through a different book every day and every morning I would return a book to select another. The library official would smile and ask "Are you certain that you are finished reading this book?" I would respond in the affirmative, adding that obviously I had very little sleep.

This might not be many people's "cup of tea" or "glass of lemonade," but it is mine. We have different interests and passions in life and that contributes to our various identities.

A DIFFERENT VIEW
OF JUDAS

We are all familiar with the gospel recordings of Judas Iscariot who betrayed our Lord, Jesus Christ. Most of us think of him as a despicable character who perpetrated such a terrible act for thirty pieces of silver. Judas was the inside connection who dealt with the enemies as he was a disciple of Jesus and he was aware of the events taking place with and around our Lord.

We should be mindful of the fact that Jesus selected Judas as one of His disciples. Just as our Lord was aware that Peter, another disciple, was going to deny even knowing Him three times before the cock crowed, so too He knew that Judas was going to betray Him, and Thomas was going to doubt His resurrection until he had a lot more evidence.

God's word says that His ways are much higher than our ways and so we need to at least attempt to look at His plan in its entirety. When we do so, what is most outstanding to us is the unconditional and indescribable love He has for us.

When I look at this master plan of God, I am reminded of the scripture, Romans 8:28 - (New Living Translation), " And we know that God causes everything to work together for the good of those who love God and are called according to his purpose for them." A very important word in that scripture is "EVERYTHING." This tells us that no matter how we perceive certain events and situations, whether they seem bad, terrible, unjust, good, great, or pleasant, our loving God is quite capable of miraculously putting them all in a melting pot and working it out to be a great outcome.

Since SALVATION is the greatest gift we can receive from God, through faith, when we look at the sequence of events from when Judas identified Jesus to the mob by kissing Him, and all the way to the resurrection of Jesus, we can clearly see that Judas played his part in God's master plan. This is why God sent His Son to us in the form of the Son of man. When Jesus was crucified by the same people He came to save, and subsequently resurrected, He returned to sit at the right hand of God to intercede for us. When He was nailed to the cross and died, He paid the price for all of our sins. God's plan is for all of us to become sons and daughters of Him.

All Jesus is asking of us, is to believe that He is our Lord and Savior through Faith in Him, and to receive His Salvation at no financial cost. If we accept His invitation genuinely, we will observe the transformation in our lives with the help of the Holy Spirit who dwells in us. We want to be followers of Jesus because of our love for Him. We aspire to be more like Him with our every Word and Deed. Does this sound too good to be true? Believe me, it is true, and it is the best path we can take for our lives.

OPEN 24/7

One of our greatest privileges in life is that we can dwell in the presence of our Lord and God any time of our choice, for as long as we wish, and we can never be turned away or receive rejection. Is that not so awesome?

To dwell in the presence of God can manifest in several different choices:-

> We can praise Him, honor Him, glorify Him, thank Him for all His blessings in our lives.

> We can lay our problems and challenges before Him and seek His guidance.

> We can seek the assistance of the Holy Spirit in the areas of our lives where we think we need to overcome weaknesses.

We can just be silent and ponder our relationship with our Lord and how fulfilling it is to have His presence in our lives.

We can ask our Lord to speak to us letting us know what He would like us to do for Him as His mouth, His hands, and His feet on this earth.

We can let our Lord know that we just love to be in His presence and to listen to what He wants to say to us.

We can ask Him for greater discernment of His will in our lives and wisdom so that we can be the most impactful ambassadors on this earth for Him.

It is extremely difficult to think of any one person on this earth who is willingly available to interact with us at any time of day or night, on any day at all, to listen to our issues, our doubts, our discomfort or any complaint we may have. On the other hand, even if we wish to thank someone for something he or she did, or congratulate someone for an achievement, or even to wish someone well, we need to seek to do so at a convenient time. We do not telephone another person at 2.a.m. in the morning when he or she is most likely asleep, to thank them or congratulate them or to convey a similar sentiment.

We should be so thankful that we can communicate with the Creator of the universe at any time of day or night, concerning any topic at all.

I dare you to top that privilege!

BIBLIOGRAPHY

Biblical quotations were taken from the King James Version and New Living Translation (as indicated).

Printed in the United States
By Bookmasters